Basic Steps

1. Fuse stabilizer to the back of the front piece of fabric.

2. Press fusible web to the back of colorful fabric pieces.

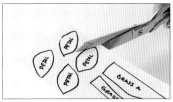

3. Trace and cut out pattern pieces from colorful fabrics.

4. Press colorful fabric pieces to the front of the post card. Optional: Topstitch or decorative stitch around pieces.

5. Layer the front (with stabilizer) to a post card back or piece of muslin. Stitch or baste around the edge to hold front and back together. Tip: Do not iron or apply heat to a printed post card back.

6. Cut around the edge so the post card is 4" x 6". To finish, Blanket stitch or zig-zag stitch around edges.

Going Places

Up, up, and away! Capture the carefree spirit with Post Cards that recall the diner you enjoyed along the way, the beautiful scenery, and the exciting experiences you will always remember. Mail these memories to friends at home and the ones you meet along the way.

instructions on pages 26 - 27

Old-Fashioned Country Charm

Primitive stitch, with its down-home, feel-good, folk art appeal is surprisingly simple to do. This post card collection offers a country look with three primitive favorites.

instructions on pages 26 and 28 - 29

Sew Much Fun

Share your love of sewing with all your guild groupies. These post cards are "sew" perfect for anyone who enjoys needle arts.

instructions on pages 29 - 30

Floral Favorites

*Say it with flowers! When words are not enough, articulate every sweet sentiment in
your heart with the gentle grace and eloquence of fabulous floral post cards.*

instructions on pages 31 - 32

Sweet Sentiments

Simple designs carry heartfelt phrases to loved ones. Express yourself with personalized pen-stitched or printed phrases.

instructions on pages 33 - 34

Awesome Appliques

Steeped in the quilting tradition of Baltimore Albums, these applique designs are an old time favorite that are oh-so-easy to reproduce on a post card.

instructions on pages 34 - 36

Perfect Patchwork

Pen-stitched patchwork post cards assemble just like puzzle pieces. These irresistible projects use up tiny scraps - just another reason post cards appeal to all who sew. Make a post card to match your latest quilted accomplishment, or create a coordinated gift post card when presenting a quilt. Any patchwork design can quickly find expression as an artful post card.

instructions on pages 36 - 37

Seasonal Joys or Holly Jolly Holidays

*Have a Holly Jolly trip to the mailbox and all your friends will too when you send these
unique post card greetings brimming with the joys of the season. Share your creativity and
holiday spirit with these fun to make and easy-to-mail post cards.*

instructions on pages 38 - 39

I wish you a Merry Christmas

Your friendship is special to me

Happy Greetings are Winging Your Way

Simple gifts are the best to receive. You will be proud to mail these delightful, heart-warming designs.

instructions on pages 40 - 41

Sassy Quilters

These designs capture us exactly the way we are - vibrant, exciting, interesting, eclectic, energetic. Share the laughter with friends on post cards that are sure to make you smile.

instructions on page 41 - 42

Tropical Dreams

Take a vacation without leaving your sewing room. Dip your toes in sandy fabrics and ocean colors. Revitalize your soul with clear blue sky colors. Whether it's sailing on the high seas or exotic tours for bird watching, you won't need to pack a thing for this grand adventure.

instructions on page 42 - 43

Favorite Things

What does your heart desire today? Allow these layered applique post cards to inspire
your creative drive toward designs that are uniquely yours.

instructions on pages 43 - 44

Springtime Elegance

Celebrate the miracles of Spring with delightful designs that are simply beautiful.
instructions on page 45

Scraps of Wisdom

I am a quilter and my house is in pieces! Capture your favorite quilter's slogan on a post card today, and remember, She who dies with the most post cards wins!.

instructions on page 46 - 47

It's Quilting Cats and Dogs!

Don't wait for a rainy day to quilt a tribute to your purr-fect pet. Put a quilter's best friend on a post card this afternoon. These designs are so simple, you can complete them in about an hour.

instructions on pages 47 - 48

Stitchin' Time

Looking for a project to share with your children or grandchildren? These easy designs are fun to make and provide that sense of accomplishment that we love so much.

instructions on pages 48 - 49

Floral Delights

Are you in the mood to applique but you don't have a lot of time? In a couple of hours you can complete a gorgeous hand-appliqued post card masterpiece. These small projects are a joy to work on and leave you feeling happy to have completed wonderful fabric art.

instructions on pages 19 and 24

YoU MAKE ME HAPPY

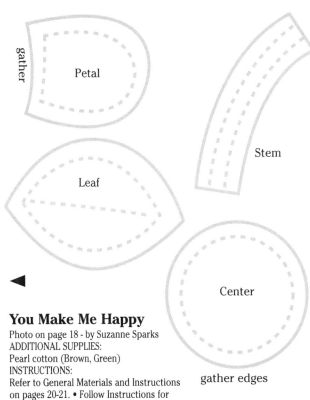

gather

Petal

Stem

Leaf

Center

gather edges

You Make Me Happy

Photo on page 18 - by Suzanne Sparks
ADDITIONAL SUPPLIES:
Pearl cotton (Brown, Green)
INSTRUCTIONS:
Refer to General Materials and Instructions
on pages 20-21. • Follow Instructions for
Applique Post Cards Needle Turn Method on page 23.
• Trace words onto background fabric. Backstitch words.
• Applique front of post card. • Embroider all details, adding French
Knots as indicated on the pattern. • Assemble post card.
• Blanket stitch around outside edges with Green pearl cotton.

Friends

Photo on page 18 - by Suzanne Sparks
ADDITIONAL SUPPLIES: Pearl cotton (Brown, Green)
INSTRUCTIONS: Refer to General Materials and Instructions on
pages 20-21. • Follow Instructions for Applique Post Cards Needle
Turn Method on page 23. • Trace words onto background fabric.
Backstitch words. • Applique front of post card. • Embroider all
details, adding French Knots as indicated on the pattern.
• Assemble post card. • Blanket stitch around outside edges with
Green pearl cotton. ▼

Petal

Center

Butterfly Wing

Body

FriEndS

Post Card

Place a Postage Stamp here

Pre-printed muslin fabric with 'Post Card' blanks printed on it for the backing is available from Design Originals.

General Materials Needed for Basic Post Cards

Scraps of cotton fabrics, muslin, wool, or felt

Stabilizer: index card, shirt weight cardboard, poster board or 70 weight Pellon

Steam-A-Seam 2 fusible web

Assorted colors including Black Micron Pigma pens, size .02 or .03

Matching threads, Pearl cotton, Embroidery floss

Embellishments: Buttons, Ribbon, Beads, Lace, Decorative thread, Diamond dust, Glass glitter

Iron and ironing board

Hot glue gun, hot glue sticks, glue stick suitable for fabric

Additional Materials (optional)

Craft and Applique Sheet

Light table

Colored pencils, crayons, acrylic paint

Mod Podge

Small paintbrush

Plastic template

Fabric sheets for inkjet printers

The Craft and Applique Sheet

The Craft and Applique Sheet is a 13" x 17" transparent, non-stick reusable sheet for all craft and pressing applications. It is very helpful for quick fuse applique and also has many other uses. It can be used under a hot glue gun to catch drips which will easily peel off and also releases paint and modeling clay. The Craft and Applique Sheet wipes off easily and rolls up for handy storage.

The Craft and Applique Sheet™ is available from www.prairiegrovepeddler.com

General Instructions

Post Cards offer a creative way to play with scraps of fabric. The finished works are lovely and useful. Send them to all your friends or display them in a quilt. You can tack stitch your post cards to a wall hanging and change them from time to time, or remove one when you need to mail it.

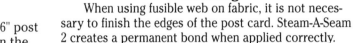

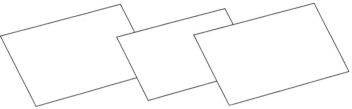

Trace two 4" x 6" onto Steam-A-Seam. Peel paper off & apply to back side of front and back fabrics.

Cut a 3½" x 5½"rectangle from stabilizer.

Place a 4" x 6" post card front on the top. Fuse with iron to assemble.

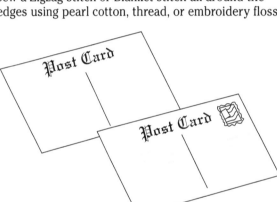

Finishing

When using fusible web on fabric, it is not necessary to finish the edges of the post card. Steam-A-Seam 2 creates a permanent bond when applied correctly.

If you prefer to finish the edges of your post card, sew a Zigzag stitch or Blanket stitch all around the edges using pearl cotton, thread, or embroidery floss.

Assembling Post Cards

METHOD 1:

1. Apply fusible web to the back side of 4" x 6" fabric pieces that will be the top and back piece.
2. Fuse 3½" x 5½" fusible web and 3½" x 5½" stabilizer to the back (sandwiching the stabilizer between front and back).
3. Decorate the front with colorful fabrics and/or embroidery.
4. Place the front piece on a muslin backing piece.

This method leaves a clean margin all around the edge, making it easier to sew around the edge with a Zigzag or decorative stitch.

METHOD 2 (No sewing required): Place two 4" x 6" pieces of fabric together with a 3½" x 5½" Stabilizer sandwiched in between.

The Stabilizer can be 70 weight Pellon or an index card.

Prepare the Back

Use a pre-printed Post Card muslin backing from *Design Originals* or print your own back.

Note: To print your own messages, use fabric sheets for inkjet printers OR press freezer paper onto one side of muslin. Then use a computer to print "Post Card" or a message on the back before assembling the card.

Use a Micron #05 Black permanent pen to write a message.

If the post card is to be mailed, print information on the back before assembling.

Be sure to remove the paper backings from Fusible web.

LAYER THE PIECES OF YOUR POST CARD AS FOLLOWS:
4" x 6" front piece, right-side-up, over the stabilizer;
center the 3½" x 5½" stabilizer piece;
4" x 6 "backing with right-side-down on the bottom.

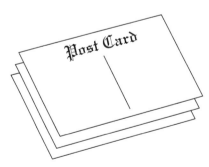

continued on page 22

Pen Stitch Post Cards

These post cards have the sentiments "stitched" with a pen.

MATERIALS FOR EACH POST CARD: Two 4" x 6" pieces of muslin for front and back • 3½" x 5½" stabilizer to be sandwiched between the front and back • Two 4" x 6" pieces fusible web for the back of each muslin piece • Black Pigma pen, size .02 or .03

Trace the templates onto clear plastic. Cut out the shapes. Use these templates to cut out the shapes after you trace the words onto the fabric.

Using a light table, trace the words onto a light color cotton fabric with a pigma pen. • Press fusible web to the back of the fabric. • Center the plastic template over the traced words and trace around the shape. Cut out inside the traced line. • Pen stitch lines ⅛" inside the outer edge. Peel paper backing off and press to post card.

Pen Stitch and Color Post Cards

Just as the name says, these post cards are "stitched" with a pen and then colored in.

MATERIALS FOR EACH POST CARD: Materials for Pen Stitch post cards plus: Crayons, colored pencils or acrylic paint • Diamond dust or glass glitter • Mod Podge • Small paintbrush

Tips: White crayons and White pencils should not be used because they do not show up well on fabric. Use White acrylic paint for all White areas of the design. Dry brush the areas you wish to paint, rather than painting them a solid color. Simply dip your brush in the paint, wipe most of it off on a paper towel and then paint.

Trace the design onto muslin front with a pigma pen. • Color the design with crayons, colored pencils or acrylic paint. • Using a paintbrush, lightly apply Mod Podge anywhere you'd like to have some glitter. Sprinkle on the glitter generously. Let dry. Shake off the excess.

ASSEMBLY:
Place fusible web on the back sides of both pieces of muslin.
Layer the card as follows: Front of the card with fusible web side up, stabilizer, muslin back with fusible web side down. Square off all edges if needed. • Press the front and back of the card so all three pieces adhere to one another. • Zigzag stitch around the edges of the card.

"Quick-As-A-Wink" Post Cards with Printed Fabrics

Post Cards with Printed Fabrics are probably the easiest and quickest to make. With no applique and no actual sewing required, you can put together something wonderful in no time at all.

Printed fabrics open a world of possibilities to the post card maker for they provide designs ranging from simply fun to elaborately artful, and you can find something appropriate for every occasion you can imagine. For those who love to hand-quilt or embroider, printed fabrics offer unexpected opportunities to add dimension and beauty to the design with simple quilting and embellishing stitches. Show off your needlecraft skills with projects that go from inspiration to completion quick as a wink.

Post Cards with Inkjet Printed Words

These post cards are made with words that are printed directly on fabric using an inkjet printer. You will need to purchase "fabric sheets for inkjet printers" which are available at many craft stores or printing/copy centers.

The instructions given for each post card will indicate the font type and size used in the project.
Follow the manufacturer's instructions for printing on the fabric sheets.
Unless otherwise instructed, apply fusible web to the back side of the printed fabric words and cut out a shape. It is very helpful to use a light box or a window so you can see the printed words when applying the fusible web to the back of the printed fabric piece.

ALTERNATIVE: If you do not wish to print the words onto fabric, you could trace the words onto muslin using a Black pigma pen, size .02 or .03.

Wool Post Cards

These post cards are fun to make because wool does not ravel, so the edges do not have to be turned under to look finished.

Each wool post card contains a front, stabilizer and back piece.
Felt may be substituted for hand-dyed wool.
Optional: Trace the patterns onto plastic template and use these templates to cut out each piece.
MATERIALS FOR EACH POST CARD: 4" x 6" wool for front of post card • 4" x 6" muslin for back of post card where the address will be written • 3½" x 5½" stabilizer • 2 pieces 4" x 6" fusible web • Assorted pieces of wool for applique • Buttons • Embroidery floss • Pearl cotton.

Trace applique patterns in reverse onto fusible web.
Press to the back side of fabric.
Cut out applique pieces.
Position appliques on the front of the card.
See individual instructions for placement, stitching and embellishments.
Return to this page when the front of the wool post card is complete.

ASSEMBLY:
METHOD 1: Press one 4" x 6" fusible web to the wrong side of the muslin back. Press the other 4" x 6" fusible web to the wrong side of the wool. Peel the paper backing off both pieces. • Lay the stabilizer on the center of the muslin and cover with the wool, sandwiching the stabilizer between the two. • Press both sides of the post card for 12-14 seconds, using a pressing cloth or Craft & Applique Sheet. Trim the edges if necessary.

METHOD 2: Cut two 4" x 6" pieces of wool for the front and back. Cut muslin 3½" x 5½" for writing on the back. Fuse 3½" x 5½" stabilizer between the 2 wool pieces. Fuse the 3½" x 5½" muslin to the back.

FINISHING:
To finish around the edges of the post card, either Blanket stitch with #5 pearl cotton or sew a Zigzag stitch.

Crazy Quilt Post Cards

If you love the look of traditional pieced designs but would rather not sew all those small pieces, you are really going to love this technique. Fusible web allows you to design extremely intricate patterns with the tiniest pieces for amazing effect. Reproduce the look of elaborate stained glass or your favorite traditional piecing.

Crazy Quilt post cards are made by backing pieces of fabric with fusible web, fitting the pieces together much like a puzzle and fusing them in place. Next, the embellishments such as buttons and lace are added. The front piece is then joined to the back, sandwiching stabilizer between. When using the patterns provided, please note that the dashed line near the edge represents the finished size of 4" x 6".
When transferring patterns onto fusible web, trace them in reverse. Label the numbers as shown on the pattern. Remove the paper backing from the side that does not have the numbers, and fuse to the fabric.

MATERIALS FOR EACH POST CARD: Two 5" x 7" pieces of muslin for front and back of post card • 3½" x 5½" stabilizer to sandwich in between the front and back • Fusible web • Fabric scraps for applique pieces

Trace the pattern in reverse onto the fusible web and fuse to fabric. Cut out the fabric pieces. Following the pattern, remove the paper backing from the fusible web and place the fabric onto 1 piece of 5" x 7" muslin.
To embellish the card, use your sewing machine or 2 strands of floss and embroidery stitches and stitch between each different piece of fabric, as on a crazy quilt.
Add any additional applique pieces.
Press the front of the card using a pressing sheet.
Sew on buttons, lace, and embellishments where required.
Hand-stitch any lettering with 2 strands of floss.
When the front of the card is completed, apply fusible web to both pieces of muslin.
Trim both pieces to 4" x 6".
Assemble post card following General Assembly Instructions on page 21.

Applique Post Cards

Whether you enjoy the relaxing peace of handwork or the exciting buzz of machine sewing, these small applique projects will send you digging out your favorite scraps for an afternoon of creative fun.

MATERIALS FOR EACH POST CARD: 4" x 6" muslin for back • 4" x 6" prequilted fabric or muslin for front • 3½" x 5½" stabilizer to sandwich in between the front and back • Fusible web • Fabric scraps for applique pieces

Trace two 4" x 6" post card outlines onto fusible web. Press one to the back side of the front fabric and the other onto the muslin backing. Cut out.

FUSING METHOD: Trace the pattern shapes in reverse onto fusible web. • Cut the pieces apart, peel paper off, and press to backs of fabrics. • Cut out applique pieces. • Using a light table, position the applique pieces on background fabric. Fuse in place.
NEEDLE TURN METHOD: Trace the pattern shapes on the back of each fabric. Cut out the pieces leaving a ⅛" border around each piece. Clip curves. Carefully press each border to the back of the fabric creating a smooth finished edge. Sew any gathers as indicated by the pattern. • Using a light table, position the applique pieces on background fabric. Pin in place. Sew around each piece with matching thread using a Blind Hem stitch.
Assemble post card following Method 1 on page 21. • Blanket stitch or Zigzag stitch around the outer edge if desired.

You Are My Sunshine

Photo on page 18 - by Suzanne Sparks

ADDITIONAL SUPPLIES:
Pearl cotton (Brown, Green)

INSTRUCTIONS:
Refer to General Materials and
Instructions on pages 20-21. • Follow
Instructions for Applique Post Cards
Needle Turn Method on page 23.
• Trace letters for words onto background
fabric. Backstitch words.
• Applique front of post card. • Embroider
all details, adding French Knots as indicated on the pattern. • Assemble
post card. • Blanket stitch around outside edges with Green pearl cotton.

Love

Photo on page 18

ADDITIONAL SUPPLIES:
Pearl cotton (Brown, Green)

INSTRUCTIONS:
Refer to General Materials and
Instructions on pages 20-21. • Follow
Instructions for Applique Post Cards
Needle Turn Method on page 23.
• Trace letters for words onto back-
ground fabric. Backstitch words.
• Applique front of post card.
• Embroider all details, adding French
Knots as indicated on the pattern.
• Assemble post card. • Blanket stitch
around outside edges with Green pearl
cotton.

Quilts Keep Friends Close ▶

Photo on page 2 -
by Suzanne Sparks

ADDITIONAL SUPPLIES:
Pearl cotton (Brown, Gold, Burgundy)

INSTRUCTIONS:
Refer to General Materials and Instructions on pages 20-21. • Follow Instructions for Crazy Quilt Post Cards on page 23. • Trace words onto background fabric. Backstitch words. Embroider all details, adding French Knots and Straight stitches as indicated on the pattern.
• Assemble post card.
• Zigzag stitch around outside edges.

Quilts Add Color to Life ▶

Photo on page 2 -
by Suzanne Sparks

ADDITIONAL SUPPLIES:
Burgundy pearl cotton

INSTRUCTIONS:
Refer to General Materials and Instructions on pages 20-21. • Follow Instructions for Crazy Quilt Post Cards on page 23. • Trace words onto front fabric. Backstitch words. • Fuse pieces in place. • Assemble post card.
• Zigzag stitch around outside edges.

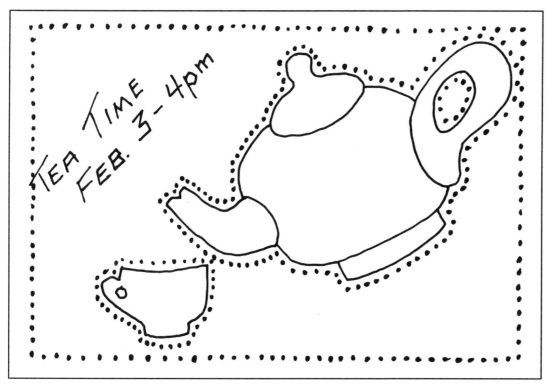

◄
Tea Time
Photo on page 4 -
by Nikki Manaffey
ADDITIONAL SUPPLIES:
4" x 6" cotton print for background
• Cotton for appliques (3" square Tan, 2" x 4" Red)
• Black Pigma pen
INSTRUCTIONS:
Refer to General Materials and Instructions on pages 20-21.
• Follow Instructions for Applique Post Cards Fusing Method on page 23. • Follow General Instructions to assemble post card. • Make Black dots around the teapot and cup and around the edge of the post card. Write "Tea Time", date and time of day.

"Quick-As-A-Wink" Printed Fabric Postcards

Do you need a card fast, but you don't want to go to the store? You want something personal, but it has to be done for the party that starts an hour from now. No need to panic. Pull out your collection of preprinted fabric scraps and make a whole cloth post card.

All you have to do is choose and fuse! You will have the perfect style to fit your occasion and you didn't even have to leave your sewing room.

We hope you enjoy these no-fuss, "done-in-no time" designs.

Waitress
Applique

◄
50's Diner
Photo on page 3 - by Pat Burnham
ADDITIONAL SUPPLIES:
4" x 6" cotton diner print for background • 3" square Black cotton for applique • Black embroidery floss • 4" x 6" cotton batting
INSTRUCTIONS:
Refer to General Materials and Instructions on pages 20-21. • Follow Instructions for Applique Post Cards Fusing Method on page 23. • Fuse batting to the back of the background. • Follow General Instructions to assemble post card. • Blanket stitch around outside edges of post card with Black floss.

Desert Cactus

Photo on page 3 - by Pat Burnham

ADDITIONAL SUPPLIES:
4" x 6" Yellow cotton for background • Cactus applique • Brown embroidery floss • 4" x 6" cotton batting

INSTRUCTIONS:
Refer to General Materials and Instructions on pages 20-21. • Zigzag stitch applique onto background. • Place batting behind the Yellow background. Quilt. • Follow General Instructions to assemble post card. • Blanket stitch around outside edges of post card with Brown floss.

Cactus
Applique

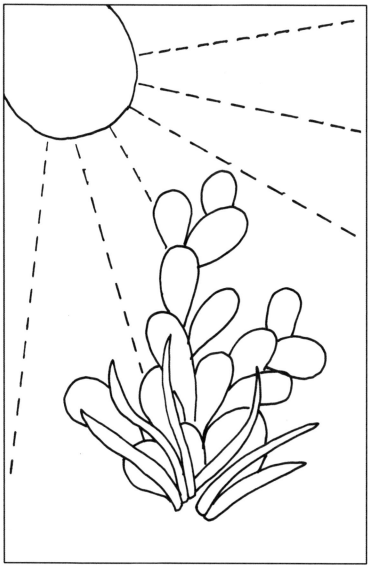

Hot Air Balloons

Photo on page 3 - by Pat Burnham

ADDITIONAL SUPPLIES:
4" x 6" cotton balloon print for background • Blue embroidery floss • 4" x 6" cotton batting

INSTRUCTIONS:
Refer to General Materials and Instructions on pages 20-21. • Place batting behind the balloon print. Quilt around clouds. • Follow General Instructions to assemble post card. • Blanket stitch around outside edges of post card with Blue floss.

◄

Long May She Wave

Photo on page 4

ADDITIONAL SUPPLIES:
4" x 6" Gold cotton for background • 3" x 3" scraps (Red, Navy, Beige, Black, Brown, Green, Gold) • Black embroidery floss • Embroidery hoop • Fine line quilter's pencil

INSTRUCTIONS:
Refer to General Materials and Instructions on pages 20-21. • Trace words onto background. Embroider words using 2 strands of Black floss. Follow Instructions for Applique Post Cards Fusing Method on page 23.
• Using 2 strands of Black floss, make a French Knot for chicken eye. Using a quilter's pencil, lightly draw legs and feet onto background fabric as shown, then embroider with 2 strands of floss.
• Follow general instructions to assemble post card. • Zigzag stitch around outside edge of card.

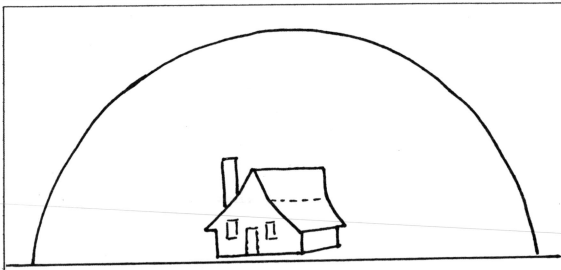

◄

Primitive old mustard moon

Photo on page 4

ADDITIONAL SUPPLIES:
4" x 6" Blue cotton fabric with stars for sky • 4" x 6" muslin for front of post card • Wool or cotton scraps (Orange or Mustard, 3 shades of Brown for the ground, house, roof; Red for chimney) • Embroidery floss (Black, Gold) • Pigma pen (Brown, Gold, Black)

INSTRUCTIONS:
Refer to General Materials and Instructions on pages 20-21. • Follow Instructions for Fusing Method of Applique Post Cards on page 23. • Zigzag stitch around all pieces. • Trace the words with a Pigma pen. • Assemble post card following Method 1 on page 21. • Zigzag stitch around the outer edges.

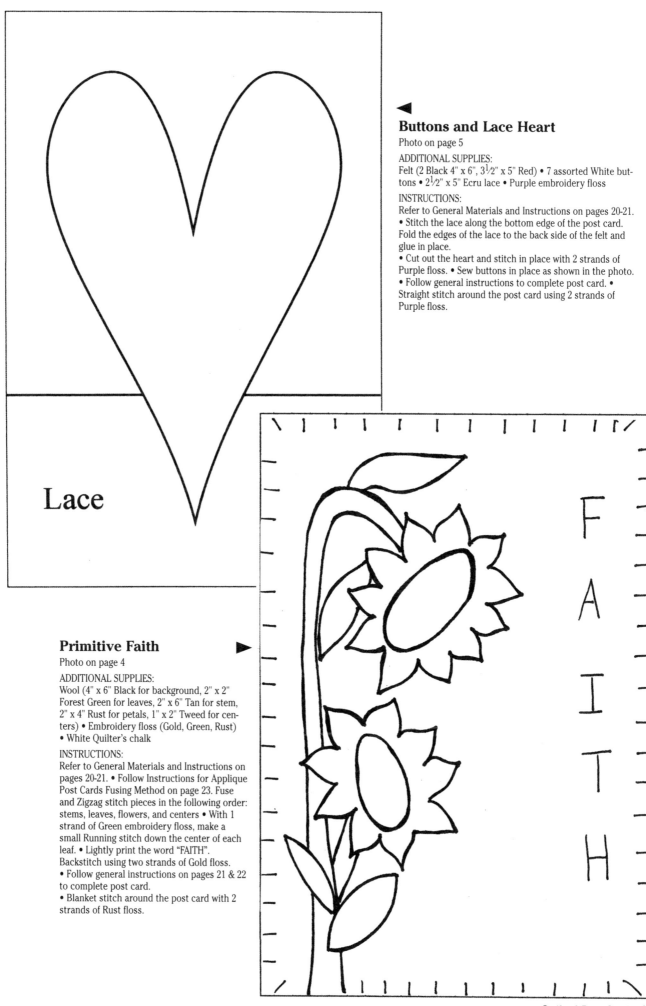

Lace

Buttons and Lace Heart
Photo on page 5

ADDITIONAL SUPPLIES:
Felt (2 Black 4" x 6", $3\frac{1}{2}$" x 5" Red) • 7 assorted White buttons • $2\frac{1}{2}$" x 5" Ecru lace • Purple embroidery floss

INSTRUCTIONS:
Refer to General Materials and Instructions on pages 20-21.
• Stitch the lace along the bottom edge of the post card. Fold the edges of the lace to the back side of the felt and glue in place.
• Cut out the heart and stitch in place with 2 strands of Purple floss. • Sew buttons in place as shown in the photo.
• Follow general instructions to complete post card. • Straight stitch around the post card using 2 strands of Purple floss.

Primitive Faith
Photo on page 4

ADDITIONAL SUPPLIES:
Wool (4" x 6" Black for background, 2" x 2" Forest Green for leaves, 2" x 6" Tan for stem, 2" x 4" Rust for petals, 1" x 2" Tweed for centers) • Embroidery floss (Gold, Green, Rust) • White Quilter's chalk

INSTRUCTIONS:
Refer to General Materials and Instructions on pages 20-21. • Follow Instructions for Applique Post Cards Fusing Method on page 23. Fuse and Zigzag stitch pieces in the following order: stems, leaves, flowers, and centers • With 1 strand of Green embroidery floss, make a small Running stitch down the center of each leaf. • Lightly print the word "FAITH". Backstitch using two strands of Gold floss.
• Follow general instructions on pages 21 & 22 to complete post card.
• Blanket stitch around the post card with 2 strands of Rust floss.

Insert 3 needles here

Tape measure goes here

Sewing Notions

Photo on page 5

ADDITIONAL SUPPLIES:
Two 4" x 6" pieces Prairie cloth backed with fusible web • 3" x 3" scraps (Red, Green, Tan, Gold, Black) • 1" x 2" Tan felt • 3 sewing or embroidery needles • Three 1/2" buttons • 4" tape measure • Black Pigma pen

INSTRUCTIONS:
Refer to General Materials and Instructions on pages 20-21. • Follow Instructions for Applique Post Cards Fusing Method on page 23. • Using the pigma pen, pen stitch the lines in the pincushion and on the spool. • Glue the tape measure in place. • Insert the 3 needles into the 1" x 2" piece of felt. Glue that felt to the top of the card. • Sew buttons in place. • Follow general instructions to complete post card. • Zigzag stitch all around the post card. • Pen stitch around the front of the card 1/8" from the edge.

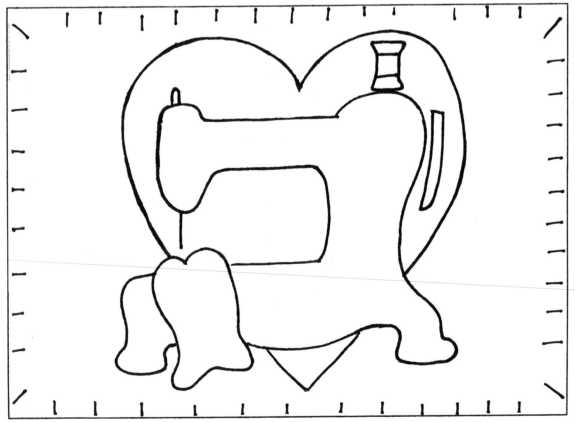

Sew in Love

Photo on page 5

ADDITIONAL SUPPLIES:
Wool (4" x 6" Ivory for background, 4" x 4" Red for heart, 4" x 4" Black for sewing machine) • Cotton scraps (1/2"x 1" Tan for spool; 1" x 2" Brown print for fabric and thread) • Embroidery floss (Gold, Black)

INSTRUCTIONS:
Refer to General Materials and Instructions on pages 20-21. • Follow Instructions for Applique Post Cards Fusing Method on page 23. • Fuse and Zigzag stitch pieces in the following order: heart, sewing machine pieces, fabric, thread spool. • Using 2 strands of Gold floss, make several long stitches for "knob" above head of machine and 1 long stitch for the needle. • Follow general instructions to complete post card. • Blanket stitch around the post card using 2 strands of Black floss.

Petals Patterns

Peach Primrose ▶

Photo on page 6

ADDITIONAL SUPPLIES:
Felt (Two 4" x 6" Light Peach, 3" x 4" Moss Green for stem and leaves, 3" squares for flower petals: Peach, Light Peach, Pale Gold) • 10 pearl 3mm beads or White floss for French Knots • Peach pearl cotton #5 • Green embroidery floss • Fabric glue

INSTRUCTIONS:
Refer to General Materials and Instructions on pages 20-21. • Cut out each of the petals, the leaves and the flower stem. Glue the stem in place. Layer the petals on top of the stem. Attach each petal by taking a few stitches through the center.
• Secure leaves in place by sewing the veins with Straight stitches and 2 strands of Green floss.
• Glue the pearls to the center of the flower, or use 6 strands of White floss to make French Knots.
• Follow general instructions to complete post card. • Sew around the edge using #5 pearl cotton and a Straight stitch.

Sweet Dreams

Photo on page 6

ADDITIONAL SUPPLIES:
1/8 yd floral background fabric • 1/8 yd Muslin for backing • 20" of lace 38" wide with one straight edge and one scalloped edge • Pigma pens (Brown, Gold, Black)

INSTRUCTIONS:
Refer to General Materials and Instructions on pages 20-21.
• Follow Instructions for Applique Post Cards Fusing Method on page 23. • Trace the words "Sweet Dreams" onto the muslin piece. Fuse and Zigzag stitch around word piece.
• Follow general instructions to complete post card. • Cut two 6" long and two 4" long pieces of lace. Position lace as shown in photo. Zigzag stitch around edges to secure.

Forget Me Not

Photo on page 6

ADDITIONAL SUPPLIES:
$\frac{1}{8}$ yd muslin • 3" x 3" scraps (Green, 2 different shades of Purple) • Embroidery floss (Dark Gray, Brown, Gold) • Embroidery hoop • Fine line quilter's pencil

INSTRUCTIONS:
Refer to General Materials and Instructions on pages 20-21. • Using a quilter's pencil, trace a 4" x 6" rectangle onto muslin. Trace the words "Forget Me Not" and flower stems. Embroider using 2 strands of floss: Gray words, Brown stems. Cut out the 4" x 6" rectangle on the traced lines. • Trace pattern pieces onto fusible web. Follow Instructions for Applique Post Cards Fusing Method on page 23. • Make 3 French Knots in the center of each flower using 2 strands of Gold floss. • Follow general instructions to assemble post card. • Zigzag stitch around outside edge of post card.

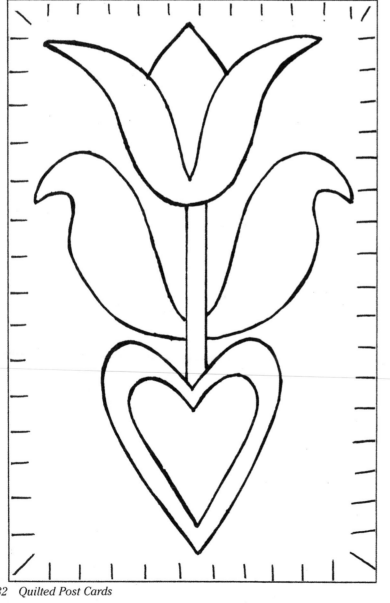

Folk Heart Tulip

Photo on page 6

ADDITIONAL SUPPLIES:
Wool ($\frac{1}{8}$ yd Ivory for background, 4" squares Green for leaves, Burgundy and Pink for flowers) • Green embroidery floss

INSTRUCTIONS:
Refer to General Materials and Instructions on pages 20-21. • Follow Instructions for Wool Post Cards on page 23. • Fuse and Zigzag around stem and leaves on background, then outer heart and tulip center, then inner heart and outer tulip • Follow general instructions to complete post card. • Using 2 strands of Green embroidery floss, Blanket stitch around outside edge of post card.

I hope you feel better soon

I Hope You Feel Better Soon

Photo on page 7

ADDITIONAL SUPPLIES:
4" x 6" Tan background fabric • 4" x 6" Muslin for backing • 2" x 2" scraps (Pink, Red, Green) • Black Pigma pen, size .03

INSTRUCTIONS:
Refer to General Materials and Instructions on pages 20-21. • Follow Instructions for Applique Post Cards Fusing Method on page 23. • Trace the words "I hope you feel better soon" and draw the stems with the Black pigma pen. • Follow general instructions to complete post card.
• Blanket stitch or zigzag stitch around the outer edge.

I enjoyed our time together

I Enjoyed Our Time Together

Photo on page 7

ADDITIONAL SUPPLIES:
⅛ yd Cream colored background fabric • 4" x 6" Muslin for backing • 2" x 2" scraps (Gold for flower center, Pink for flowers, Green for leaves) • Black Pigma pen, size .03

INSTRUCTIONS:
Refer to General Materials and Instructions on pages 20-21.
• Follow Instructions for Post cards with Inkjet Printed Words on page 22.
• Print words on Cream background in Bodoni MT Condensed font, size 60. Follow Instructions for Applique Post Cards Fusing Method on page 23. • Trace the stem using the Black pigma pen. • Blanket stitch or Zigzag stitch around the outer edge.

Come join

the party

◄

Come Join the Party
Photo on page 7

ADDITIONAL SUPPLIES:
4" x 6" Tan background fabric • 4" x 6" Muslin for backing • 3" x 3" scraps (Pink, Brown print, Green) • Black Pigma pen, size .03

INSTRUCTIONS:
Refer to General Materials and Instructions on pages 20-21. • Follow Instructions for Applique Post Cards Fusing Method on page 23.
• Trace the words "Come join the party" and draw the stem with a Black pigma pen. • Follow general instructions to complete post card.
• Blanket stitch or Zigzag stitch around the outer edge.

Swamp Rose ►
Photo on page 8

ADDITIONAL SUPPLIES:
4" x 6" Pink background fabric • 4" x 6" Muslin (for backing) • 4" x 4" scraps (Pink for flowers, Green for circle, Light Green for leaves, Tan for square) • Black Pigma pen, size .03

INSTRUCTIONS:
Refer to General Materials and Instructions on pages 20-21. • Follow Instructions for Applique Post Cards Fusing Method on page 23.
• Make dots in the center of each flower. • Follow General Instructions to complete post card. • Blanket stitch or Zigzag stitch around the outer edge.

Bell Flowers ▶

Photo on page 8

ADDITIONAL SUPPLIES:
4" x 6" Purple background fabric • 4" x 6" Muslin for backing • 4" x 4" scraps (Green for leaves, 2 Purples for flowers and circle, Tan for square)

INSTRUCTIONS:
Refer to General Materials and Instructions on pages 20-21. • Follow Instructions for Applique Post Cards Fusing Method on page 23. • Follow general instructions to complete post card. • Blanket stitch or Zigzag stitch around the outer edge.

Sundrops ▶

Photo on page 8

ADDITIONAL SUPPLIES:
4" x 6" Gold fabric for front • 4" x 6" Muslin for backing • 4" x 4" scraps (Gold, 2 Tans, Green) • Black Pigma pen, size .03

INSTRUCTIONS:
Refer to General Materials and Instructions on pages 20-21. • Follow Instructions for Applique Post Cards Fusing Method on page 23. • Make stitch marks and dots on flowers with a Black pigma pen. • Follow General Instructions to complete post card. • Blanket stitch or Zigzag stitch around the outer edge.

Tulip Wreath

Photo on page 8

ADDITIONAL SUPPLIES:
4" x 6" Blue background fabric • 4" x 6" Muslin for backing • 4" x 4" scraps
(2 Blue, Tan)

INSTRUCTIONS:
Refer to General Materials and Instructions on pages 20-21. • Follow
Instructions for Applique Post Cards Fusing Method on page 23. • Follow
General Instructions to complete post card. • Blanket stitch or Zigzag stitch
around the outer edge.

Leaf ▶

Photo on page 9

ADDITIONAL SUPPLIES:
4" x 6" Orange background fabric • 4" x 6" Muslin for backing
• 4" x 4" scrap of Dark Red • Black Pigma Pen, size .03

INSTRUCTIONS:
Refer to General Materials and Instructions on pages 20-21.
• Follow Instructions for Applique Post Cards Fusing Method
on page 23. • Fuse pieces in the following order: Red square,
Orange squares and triangles. • Make stitch marks around the
Orange squares and triangles with a Black pigma pen.
• Follow general instructions to complete post card. • Blanket
stitch or Zigzag stitch around the outer edge.

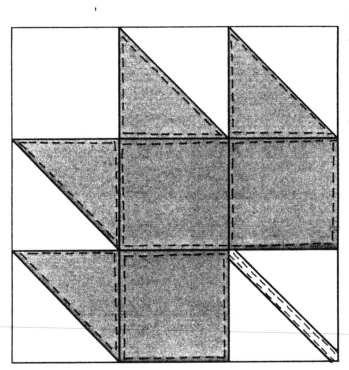

Star ▶

Photo on page 9

ADDITIONAL SUPPLIES:
4" x 6" Black background fabric • 4" x 6" Muslin for backing • 8 different 2" x 2" scraps • Black Pigma pen, size .03

INSTRUCTIONS:
Refer to General Materials and Instructions on pages 20-21. • Follow Instructions for Applique Post Cards Fusing Method on page 23. • Make stitch marks around each triangle using the Black pigma pen. • Follow general instructions to complete post card. • Blanket stitch or Zigzag stitch around the outer edge.

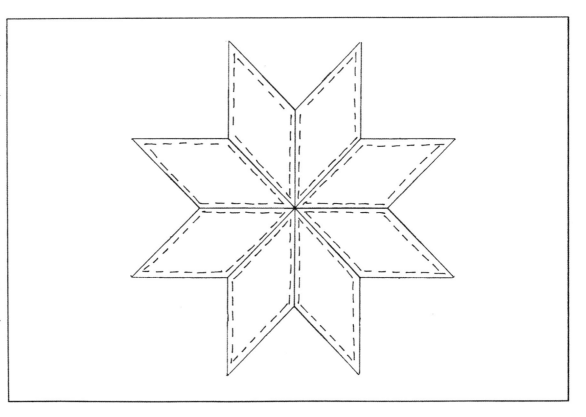

Poinsettia ▶

Photo on page 9

ADDITIONAL SUPPLIES:
4" x 6" Red background fabric • 4" x 6" Muslin for backing • 4" x 4" scraps (1 Green, 2 Reds)

INSTRUCTIONS:
Refer to General Materials and Instructions on pages 20-21. • Follow Instructions for Crazy Quilt Post Cards on page 23. • Follow General Instructions to complete post card. • Blanket stitch or Zigzag stitch around the outer edge.

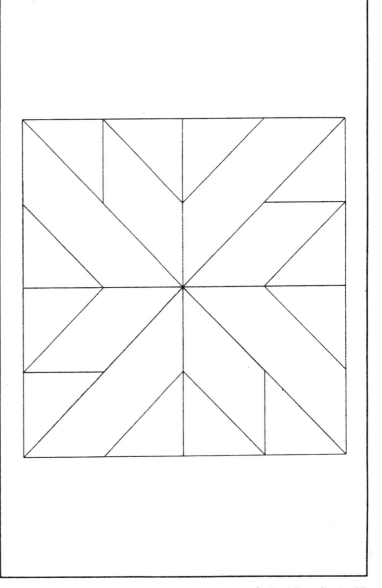

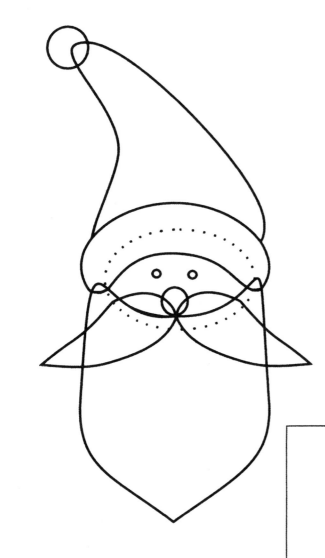

◄

Santa

Photo on page 10

ADDITIONAL SUPPLIES:
Felt (Two 4" x 6" Black, 1" x 2" Tan or Light Pink for face, $\frac{1}{2}$" x $\frac{1}{2}$" Rose for nose, 3" x 3" Red for hat, 3" x 4" White for hat brim, pompom, mustache, beard) • Pearl cotton #5 (Black, Gold) • Diamond Dust or glass glitter • Mod Podge • Paintbrush

INSTRUCTIONS:
Refer to General Materials and Instructions on pages 20-21. • Follow Instructions for Applique Post Cards Fusing Method on page 23. • The dotted lines seen in the hat brim and on the beard are the cutting lines for the face. Fuse pieces in the following order: face, hat, beard, hat brim, nose, mustache pieces, and pompom on the tip of the hat. • Using the pearl cotton, make a French Knot for each eye. • Follow general instructions to complete post card. • Blanket stitch around the post card with Gold pearl cotton. • Brush Mod Podge where you'd like the glitter to be and then sprinkle it on. Let dry. Shake off the excess glitter.

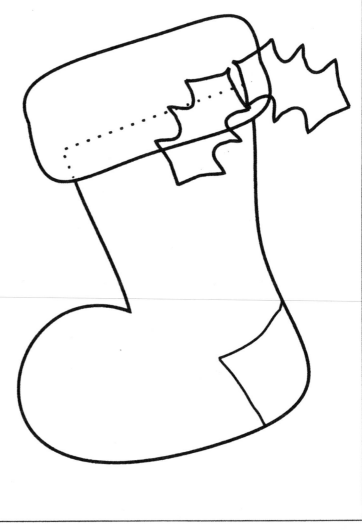

Stocking   ►

Photo on page 10

ADDITIONAL SUPPLIES:
Felt (Two 4" x 6" Sage, 3" x 4" Red for stocking, 2" x 4" White for cuff and heel, 2" x 3" Green for holly) • Pearl cotton (Red, Green)

INSTRUCTIONS:
Refer to General Materials and Instructions on pages 20-21.
• Follow Instructions for Applique Post Cards Fusing Method on page 23. Straight stitch the Red stocking to the Sage background using Red pearl cotton. • Position the cuff and the heel. Attach them with a Straight stitch using Red pearl cotton. • Attach leaves with a Straight stitch up the center of each holly leaf using Green pearl cotton. • Make berries with 3 French Knots using Red pearl cotton. • Follow general instructions to complete post card. • Straight stitch around the post card using Green pearl cotton.

Snowman ▶

Photo on page 10

ADDITIONAL SUPPLIES:
Felt (2 pieces Blue 4" x 6", Black 2" x 3" for hat, Red 1" x 3" for hat brim and scarf, White 2" x 3" for face, Orange $\frac{1}{2}$" x 1" for nose) • $\frac{3}{8}$" star button • Embroidery floss (Black, White, Green, Gold)

INSTRUCTIONS:
Refer to General Materials and Instructions on pages 20-21.
• Follow Instructions for Applique Post Cards Fusing Method. • Blanket stitch around the hat with 2 strands of Black floss. • Stitch the mouth using 3 strands of Black floss. Make the eyes with French Knots using 6 strands of Black floss. Sew a straight stitch around the hat brim and scarf using 2 strands of Green floss. • Sew the star button to the hat brim. • To make snowflakes all over the front of the card, use 2 strands of White floss to make three $\frac{3}{8}$" long Straight stitches that intersect in the middle.
• Follow general instructions to complete post card.
• Blanket stitch around the post card using 2 strands of White floss.

Gingerbread Star ▶

Photo on page 10

ADDITIONAL SUPPLIES:
Felt (2 pieces of Black 4" x 6", 2 Green strips $\frac{1}{2}$" x 4", 2 Red strips $\frac{1}{2}$" x 6", $3\frac{1}{2}$" square Tan for star) • Red pearl cotton #5 • $\frac{5}{8}$" button • Mod Podge • Diamond Dust or glass glitter

INSTRUCTIONS:
Refer to General Materials and Instructions on pages 20-21. • Follow Instructions for Applique Post Cards on page 23. Fuse the Red and Green felt strips as shown in photo, then fuse the star. • Tie the button to the center of the star using Red pearl cotton. • Follow general instructions to complete post card. • Blanket stitch around the edge with Red pearl cotton. • Paint the star with Mod Podge and sprinkle Diamond Dust or glass glitter. Let dry. Shake off excess glitter.

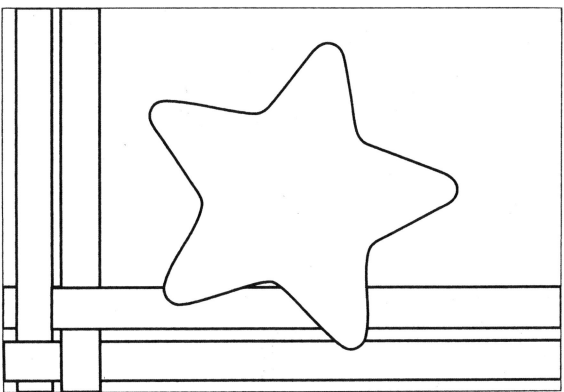

◀

I Wish You a Merry Christmas

Photo on page 11

ADDITIONAL SUPPLIES:
$\frac{1}{8}$ yd Cream colored background fabric • $\frac{1}{8}$ yd Muslin for backing • Scraps (Gold 1" x 1" for star, Brown 1" x 2" for trunk, Green 3" x 4" for tree)

INSTRUCTIONS:
Refer to General Materials and Instructions on pages 20-21. • Follow Instructions for Post cards with Inkjet Printed Words on page 22. • Print words on fabric sheet using Bodoni MT Condensed font, size 50 or trace words using a Black pigma pen. • Follow Instructions for Applique Post Cards Fusing Method on page 23. • Blanket stitch or Zigzag stitch around the outer edge.

◀

Your Friendship is Special to Me

Photo on page 11

ADDITIONAL SUPPLIES:
$\frac{1}{8}$ yd Cream colored background fabric • $\frac{1}{8}$ yd Muslin for backing • Scraps (Gold for beak, Black for eye, 2 Reds for body and wing, Green for leaves) • Black Pigma pen, size .03 • Correction fluid

INSTRUCTIONS:
Refer to General Materials and Instructions on pages 20-21. • Follow Instructions for Post Cards with Inkjet Printed Words on page 22. • Print words on fabric sheet using Century Schoolbook font, size 36 or trace words using a Black pigma pen. • Follow Instructions for Applique Post Cards Fusing Method on page 23. • Trace the stem using the Black pigma pen. • Blanket stitch or Zigzag stitch around the outer edge. • Using correction fluid, make a small dot on the eye. Let dry.

Feather Your Nest

Photo on page 11

ADDITIONAL SUPPLIES:
Wool (1/8 yd Tan for background, Dark Brown 4" x 5" for trees, Light Brown 4" x 6" for branches, 1" square Green for leaves, 1" square Black and Gold for beaks, 2 shades of Red 3" x 4" for birds) • Embroidery floss (Black for stems, Ecru for eyes) • Black Pigma pen

INSTRUCTIONS:
Refer to General Materials and Instructions on pages 20-21. • Follow Instructions for Applique Post Cards Fusing Method on page 23. • Write the words "Feather Your Nest" on the limb with a Black pigma pen. • Fuse pieces in the following order: large trees, birds, smaller limb, larger limb with words, Black mask on the larger bird, bird beaks, and leaves. • Using 2 strands of floss, Stem stitch Black stems and make a French Knot with Ecru floss for eyes on birds. • Using Black pigma pen, draw feet for each bird. • Follow general instructions to complete post card. • Zigzag stitch around outside edges of post card.

Blessed Is She

Photo on page 12

ADDITIONAL SUPPLIES:
1/8 yd Gray wool or cotton for background • Black wool for oval • Cotton scraps (muslin for face, Gray for words, solid Pink for blouse and flower, Brown for hair, Pink print for halo) • Seed beads (2 Green, 1 Red) • Pink pearl cotton or embroidery floss • Pigma pens (Black, Brown, Red)

INSTRUCTIONS:
Refer to General Materials and Instructions on pages 20-21. • From background fabric, cut a 4" x 6" rectangle. • Follow Instructions for Post Cards with Inkjet Printed Words on page 22. • Print words using Abadi MT Condensed font size 22 italics, or trace words using a Black pigma pen. • Position words on background fabric and press in place. • Zigzag stitch around word pieces. • See Instructions for Applique Post Cards Fusing Method on page 23. Zigzag stitch around oval. • Using a Black pigma pen, trace or draw eyes, lashes, brows, pupils, nose, and a faint chin line onto front of face piece. Trace or draw mouth with Red pigma pen. • With Green floss, make a French Knot in center of flower. Sew a Green bead at each ear for earrings and a tiny Red bead at neckline or make French Knots in place of beads. • Zigzag stitch around fused pieces. • Follow General Instructions to assemble post card. • Blanket stitch around outside edge of post card with Pink pearl cotton.

WE'RE QUITE THE PAIR

▲

We're Quite the Pair

Photo on page 12

ADDITIONAL SUPPLIES:
1/8 yd Pink fabric for background • Scraps (solid Black, Black-White print) • Black Pigma pen

INSTRUCTIONS:
Refer to General Materials and Instructions on pages 20-21. • Follow Instructions for Post Cards with Inkjet Printed Words on page 22. Print words on background fabric in Engravers MT font size 42 or trace words using a Black pigma pen. • See Instructions for Applique Post Cards Fusing Method on page 23. • Follow general instructions to complete post card. • Zigzag stitch around outside edges of post card.

▲

The Pink Flamingo

Photo on page 12

ADDITIONAL SUPPLIES:
4" x 6" muslin for background • 4" x 6" Pink cotton • Pigma pen (Brown, Black) • Green colored pencil

INSTRUCTIONS:
Refer to General Materials and Instructions on pages 20-21. • Follow Pen Stitch and Color Instructions on page 22. • Trace the flamingo onto Pink fabric. Draw all dashed lines and face with a Black pigma pen. Cut out. • Trace the stems and leaves onto muslin. Fill the leaves in using the Green colored pencil. • Follow General Instructions to assemble and finish post card. • Zigzag stitch around outside edge of post card.

On Vacation

Photo on page 12

ADDITIONAL SUPPLIES:
1/8 yd Blue cotton (Sky print for background, Water print) • 3" x 3" scraps (3 shades of Green, Purple, Black, Orange, Yellow, Red) • Black embroidery floss or pearl cotton • Black Pigma pen

INSTRUCTIONS:
Refer to General Materials and Instructions on pages 20-21. • From "sky" fabric, cut a 4" x 6" rectangle. Trace the words onto background fabric with a pigma pen. Alternate words: "The sky is Blue, The sand is hot, Wish you were here, I miss you a lot." • Follow Instructions for Applique Post Cards Fusing Method on page 23. • Using Black pearl cotton or floss, make one long stitch from top to bottom of boat sail and make a French Knot at top of umbrella. • Follow general instructions to assemble post card. • Zigzag stitch around outside edges of post card.

The sky is blue, The sand is hot, Sometimes I miss you, And sometimes not.

Summer Flower

Photo on page 13 - by Pat Burnham

ADDITIONAL SUPPLIES:
4" x 6" White cotton for background • Applique fabrics (4" x 4" Orange, 1" x 1" Purple, 1" x 3" Dark Green, 2" x 5" Light Green) • Embroidery floss (Yellow, Green, Rust) • 4" x 6" cotton batting

INSTRUCTIONS:
Refer to General Materials and Instructions on pages 20-21. • Follow Instructions for Applique Post Cards Needle Turn Method on page 23. • Trace swirl pattern onto Light Green fabric. Backstitch with Green floss. • Applique pieces in the following order: stem, flower, flower center, Green swirl piece. • Fuse batting to the back of the applique. • Follow General Instructions to assemble post card. • Blanket stitch around outside edges of post card with Green and Rust floss.

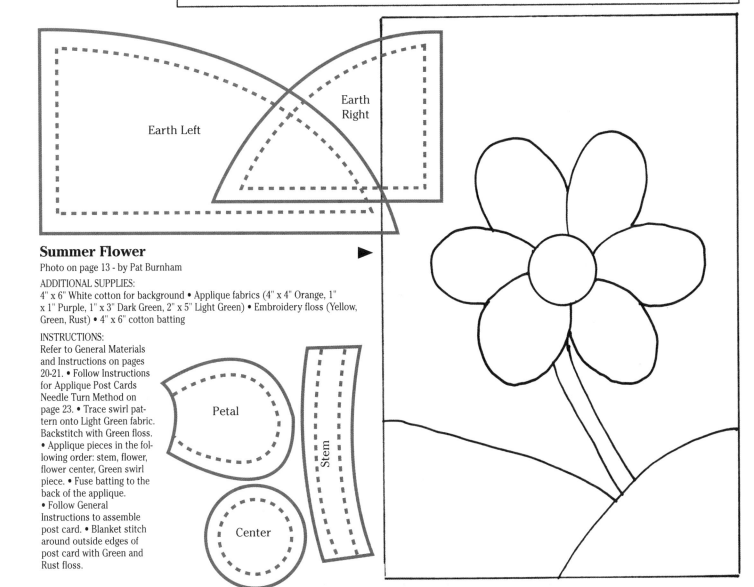

Earth Left

Earth Right

Petal

Stem

Center

Tickled Pink

Photo on page 13

ADDITIONAL SUPPLIES:
4" x 6" Green wool felt, wool, or cotton fabric for background • Scraps (Pink, Black, Muslin) • Black embroidery floss • Ecru pearl cotton or floss • Black Pigma pen

INSTRUCTIONS:
Refer to General Materials and Instructions on pages 20-21. • Follow Instructions for Applique Post Cards Fusing Method on page 23. Using 2 strands of Black floss, make 4 French Knots as shown down center of dress top. • Follow Instructions for Post Cards with Inkjet Printed Words on page 22. Print words in Comic Sans MS font size 18 or trace words using a Black pigma pen. • Trace outline of tag piece around printed words and cut out. Fuse tag in place. • Using Ecru pearl cotton, make 2 long stitches for the "tag string". • To assemble, follow Instructions for Wool Post Cards on page 23. • Using Black floss, Blanket stitch around outside edge of post card.

Let's Shop 'til We Drop

Photo on page 13

ADDITIONAL SUPPLIES:
4" x 6" Bright Pink fabric for background • $1/8$ yd White fabric • 3" x 3" scraps (3 different Pink) • Black pearl cotton • Black Pigma pen

INSTRUCTIONS:
Refer to General Materials and Instructions on pages 20-21. • Follow Instructions for Post cards with Inkjet Printed Words on page 22. • Print words on fabric sheet using Space Toaster font size 36 or trace words using a Black pigma pen. • Follow Instructions for Applique Post Cards Fusing Method on page 23. • Stitch strings and bows on packages using one strand of Black pearl cotton. • Follow general instructions to assemble post card. • Zigzag stitch around outside edges of post card.

Decorative Egg ▶

Photo on page 14

ADDITIONAL SUPPLIES:
Felt (2 Purple 4" x 6", Light Peach 3" x 4½" for egg, Green 1" x 1" for leaves) • 1" x 4" lace • Two 3½" lengths pearl trim • ⅜" x 2½" Gold trim • 8" Gold cord for bow • Silk roses (Two ⅜", One ⅝") • Ecru pearl cotton #5 • Fabric glue

INSTRUCTIONS:
Refer to General Materials and Instructions on pages 20-21. • Glue Gold trim and lace to the egg as shown in photo. Fold the excess to the back and glue in place.• Glue 2 lengths of pearl trim along the top edge of the lace. • Tie a small bow with Gold cord and glue it to the center front of the lace. • Cut out tiny Green leaves. Glue the leaves and flowers in place. • Glue the egg to the front of the post card. • Fuse the muslin onto the back of the post card. • Follow general instructions to complete post card. • Blanket stitch all along the edge using Ecru pearl cotton.

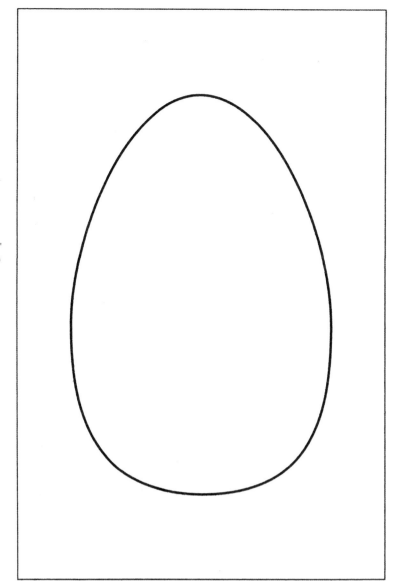

Dove of Hope ▼

Photo on page 14

ADDITIONAL SUPPLIES:
Wool (4" x 6" Pink for background, 4" x 6" Ivory for dove, 1" square Olive Green for leaves, ½" square Gray for beak) • Embroidery floss (Olive Green, Black) • Quilter's pencil

INSTRUCTIONS:
Refer to General Materials and Instructions on pages 20-21. • Follow Instructions for Applique Post Cards Fusing Method on page 23. Position, fuse and Zigzag stitch around upper wing, then do the same for the body and beak. Position forward wing. Press in place. Zigzag stitch around wing. • Using 2 strands of Black floss, make a French Knot for dove's eye. With a quilter's pencil, print the word "Hope" as shown. With 2 strands of Olive Green floss, Backstitch words and the olive branch. • Fuse leaves at upper end of olive branch. • Follow general instructions to complete post card. • Zigzag stitch around outside edge of post card.

Quilts
Are Pieced
with Love

▲ Quilted Words of Wisdom ▼

Photo on page 15 - by Suzanne Sparks

ADDITIONAL SUPPLIES:
Pearl cotton (Burgundy, Green)

INSTRUCTIONS:
Refer to General Materials and Instructions on pages 20-21. • Follow Instructions for Crazy Quilt Post Cards on page 23. • Trace letters for words onto background fabric. Backstitch words with pearl cotton. • Assemble post card. • Zigzag stitch around outside edges.

When Life
Hands You
Scraps, Make
a Quilt.

Fill Your Cabin with Quilts

Photo on page 15 - by Suzanne Sparks

ADDITIONAL SUPPLIES: Burgundy pearl cotton

INSTRUCTIONS: Refer to General Materials and Instructions on pages 20-21. • Follow Instructions for Crazy Quilt Post Cards on page 23. • Trace words onto background fabric. Backstitch words with pearl cotton.
• Assemble post card.
• Zigzag stitch around outside edges.

Cut fringe through all 4 layers.

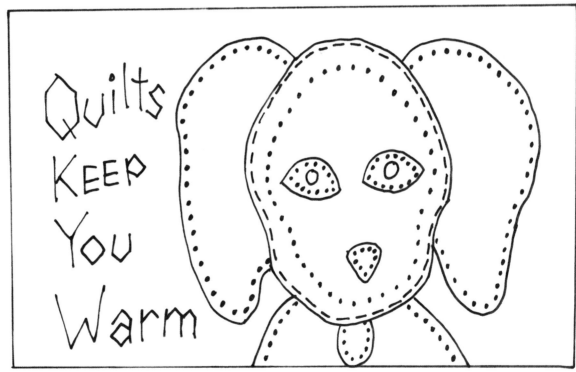

Quilts Keep You Warm

Photo on page 16 - by Suzanne Sparks

ADDITIONAL SUPPLIES:
Squares of cotton print fabric (3" Red, 2" Tan, 8" Brown for 5 faces and 1 body) • Pearl cotton (Burgundy, Black)

INSTRUCTIONS:
Refer to General Materials and Instructions on pages 20-21. • Follow Instructions for Crazy Quilt Post Cards Fusing Method on page 23. • Fuse ears, 1 face, body, and tongue to front of post card. Sew a Running stitch around each piece. • Trace words onto front fabric. Backstitch words with Burgundy pearl cotton. • Stack additional face pieces on top of fused face. Sew a Running stitch $1/4$" from the edge. Fuse eyes and nose in place. Sew a Running stitch around eyes and nose. Using Black pearl cotton, make pupils of eyes with 4 small Satin stitches. Clip all around the face to create fringe. • Assemble post card. • Zigzag stitch around outside edges.

Cut fringe through all 4 layers.

Cats and Quilts are Cozy

Photo on page 16 - by Suzanne Sparks

ADDITIONAL SUPPLIES:
Squares of cotton print fabric (3" Red, 2" White, 1" White, 8" Brown for 5 cat faces and 1 body) • Pearl cotton (Gold, Green, Black)

INSTRUCTIONS:
Refer to General Materials and Instructions on pages 20-21. • Follow Instructions for Crazy Quilt Post Cards Fusing Method on page 23.
• Fuse ears, 1 face, body, and collar to front of post card. Sew a Running stitch around each piece. • Trace words onto front fabric. Backstitch words with Gold pearl cotton. • Stack additional face pieces on top of fused face. Sew a Running stitch $1/4$" from the edge. Fuse eyes and nose in place. Sew a Running stitch around eyes and nose. Using Green pearl cotton, make pupils of eyes with 4 small Satin stitches. Clip all around the face to create fringe. • Embroider face details with Black pearl cotton. • Assemble post card. • Zigzag stitch around outside edges.

My Flag

Photo on page 17 - by Judy Linn

ADDITIONAL SUPPLIES:
4" x 6" tea dyed muslin • Embroidery floss (Brown, Blue, Red, Yellow)

INSTRUCTIONS:
Refer to General Materials and Instructions on pages 20-21. • Trace pattern onto muslin. Backstitch design and words. • Zigzag stitch around outside edges of post card.

Beribboned Blue Heart ▶

Photo on page 17

ADDITIONAL SUPPLIES:
Felt (2 Light Blue 4" x 6", Dark Blue 4" square for heart) • 8" White ⅝" wide trim • 12" White ⅛" wide ribbon • White pearl cotton #5 • Fabric glue

INSTRUCTIONS
Refer to General Materials and Instructions on pages 20-21. • Blanket stitch the heart in place. • Straight stitch all the way around the heart, about ½" from the edge. • Tie a ribbon bow. Glue to the front of the heart. • Glue the White trim in place. • Follow general instructions to complete post card. • Blanket stitch around the card with White pearl cotton.

Button Collection ▶

Photo on page 17

ADDITIONAL SUPPLIES:
Two pieces of Black felt 4" x 6" • 15 assorted buttons ¾" diameter • Gold pearl cotton #5 • Black sewing thread

INSTRUCTIONS:
Refer to General Materials and Instructions on pages 20-21. • Using the pattern provided, cut the scalloped edged front and back from Black felt. • Sew the buttons to the front of the post card. • Follow general instructions to complete post card.
• Blanket stitch around the post card with Gold pearl cotton.

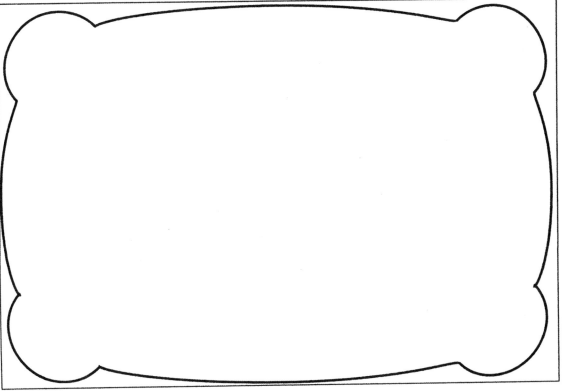

Post Cards Quilt
Small Wall Hanging with Pockets
photo on quilt page 51 - photo of Post Cards on page 18

FINISHED SIZE: 18" x 20"
MATERIALS:
⅔ yard White pre-quilted print for center block and backing
⅛ yard Pink for inner border
¼ yard Green for outer border and binding

CUTTING:
Center block
1   13½" x 15½"

Pink Inner Border
2 strips   1" x 15½" for sides
2 strips   1" x 14½" for top and bottom

Green Outer Border
2 strips   2½" x 16½" for sides
2 strips   2½" x 18½" for top and bottom

BACKING
1   19" x 21"

BINDING:
Cut 2" strips and sew together for 80".

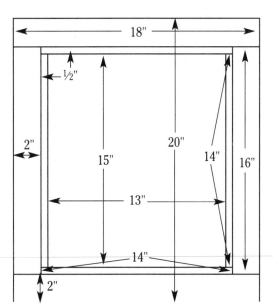

Assembly

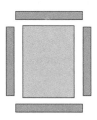 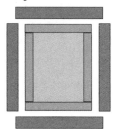

1. Add inner borders.   **2.** Add outer borders.

INSTRUCTIONS:
1. Sew the Pink 1" x 15½" side strips to the center block.
2. Sew the Pink 1" x 14½" strips to the top and bottom.
3. Sew the Green 2½" x 16½" strips to each side.
4. Sew the Green 2½" x 18½" strips to top and bottom.
5. Layer the top and backing with wrong sides together.
6. Quilt as desired.
7. Sew binding in place following Finishing and Binding Instructions.

Finishing and Binding

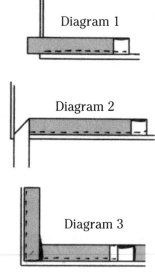

Diagram 1

Diagram 2

Diagram 3

INSTRUCTIONS:
1. Trim the edges in line with the quilt top.
2. Lay binding face down along the front edge of the quilt top and pin.
3. Fold binding in half lengthwise. Press.
4. See Diagram 1. Sew binding to quilt with a ¼" seam.
5. When you come to the corner, fold down, then up and pin. See Diagram 2.
6. See Diagram 3. Overlap the binding ends.
7. Fold binding over to the back and pin.
8. Tuck under the edge and handstitch to secure.

SUPPLIERS - Most craft and variety stores carry an excellent assortment of supplies. If you need something special, ask your local store to contact the following companies:
POST CARD BACKING FABRIC
    Design Originals
STEAM-A-SEAM 2 FUSIBLE WEB
    The Warm Company

PELLON
    Pellon
CRAFT & APPLIQUE SHEET
    Prairie Grove Peddler
EMBROIDERY FLOSS
& PEARL COTTON
    DMC
    Weeks Dye Works

MANY THANKS to my friends for their cheerful help and wonderful ideas!
Kathy McMillan • Janet Long
Donna Kinsey • Diana McMillan
David & Donna Thomason